www.finishinglinepress.com

When Mockingbirds Sing

poems by

Katherine Nelson-Born

Finishing Line Press
Georgetown, Kentucky

When Mockingbirds Sing

ACKNOWLEDGMENTS

Katherine Nelson-Born extends grateful acknowledgment to the advisors, editors,
publishers and judges for the following organizations, journals, periodicals, and
anthologies that published or otherwise honored the below poems or earlier versions of
them now being published collectively in *When Mockingbirds Sing*.

Agnes Scott College Writer's Festival (1994): When Geese Fly South. Finalist in Writers'
Festival Competition.
Alabama Writers Conclave (AWC) 2015: Return to Palmyra. Honorable Mention, Writers'
Competition, judged by Vivian Shipley, July 2015, Fairhope, AL, published in annual
journal, *ALALIT*, Fall 2015, http://alalit.com/
Alyss (2016): Finding the Way Back. Issue Tre, http://alysslit.com/.
Ellipsis (1990): Year of the Rat.
Emerald Coast Review XVIII (2015): https://sites.google.com/site/wflfonline/submissions
– After Breakfast; Fresh Cuttings; One Palmyra Christmas.
Emerald Coast Review XV (2009): When Mockingbirds Sing
Emerald Coast Review XII (2005): Me, Camille, and Mr. Black.
Excelsior ReView (2013): Falling Up. Excelsior College, NY, http://review.excelsior.edu/
Maple Leaf Rag 15th Anniversary Anthology (1994): Epiphany in Mississippi.
Penumbra (1996): The Geometry of Your Bones; A Stone's Throw.
Tennessee Williams/New Orleans Literary Festival (1990) — Ellipsis Award for Poetry, 24
April 1990, University of New Orleans: Year of the Rat

Publisher: Leah Maines
Editor: Christen Kincaid
Cover Art: Ryn Holmes
Author Photo: Rowan E. Born
Cover Design: Elizabeth Maines

Printed in the USA on acid-free paper.
Order online: www.finishinglinepress.com
also available on amazon.com

Author inquiries and mail orders:
Finishing Line Press
P. O. Box 1626
Georgetown, Kentucky 40324
U. S. A.

Table of Contents

Poetry is like a bird, it ignores all frontiers.

–Yevgeny Yevtushenko

When Mockingbirds Sing

The crickets cheer the sun's descent into the lake.
The sky yawns and swallows the sun's cherry-red
globe sliced with orange, like candy in a child's mouth—
absorbing the shrinking orb until the last
sliver slides down into throaty darkness.
All that is left is the sweet afterglow.
A few stray chirps, then silence grows
until in the blue-black velvet a call comes.
Some call it a catbird. Some think it's a sin
to shoot one. They make music and bother
no one, except cats, perhaps, who have it coming
anyway. I think they mock me. I sit here
working to make words sing when they sing
without effort. So perfectly do mockingbirds mimic
other birdsong, the human ear cannot tell the difference.
So sweet, their mocking seems the real thing,
like a knock-off Gucci bag at an Italian market,
so beautiful a mimicry, who cares?
Like soft Italian leather, the *burra burra* of
the bluebird, the blush of the setting sun,
the mockingbird's music mesmerizes.
I trip over each word, tempted to drop the pen,
listen more to the music of the spheres, and dream
I can sing like the mockingbird of a time
older than the ruins of Pompeii,
newer than the morning of a day not yet born.

After Breakfast

Breakfast—apples, apricots, and oatmeal,
the spoon released to your chubby fingers,
you direct your first symphony.
Oatmeal faced, Daughter, you are
so eager to indulge
in *everything*.

The sun draws us to the back porch,
light streaking through the screen
like God's fingers caressing
where I stand sun-kissed
with you at my knees,
open-mouthed with delight.

Silver globes in the sun,
the bright bubbles I blow,
I present to you on my wand.
Your fingers burst every one,
you—amazed each time
the shining orbs
disappear at your touch.
Even when you kiss them,
poof, they're gone.

You look at me, a question
in your eyes. Galaxies
expand and vanish.

I give you silver
soap bubbles.

Finding the Way Back

(Inspired by Robert M. Edsel's The Monuments Men: Allied Heroes, Nazi Thieves, and the Greatest Treasure Hunt in History)

Mona Lisa smiles down the barrel of a German Luger.
The question: Is art worth a life?

Stacked head high in a salt mine
five thousand bells bear silent witness
next to barrels of gold fillings
extracted from humans alive or dead.
Auschwitz. Buchenwald. Ashes in the wind
covered the head of my grandfather.
Unlike Mona Lisa's smile,
there is no photograph surviving the war,
no painting to which to point,
to show you, Daughter. Here is your heritage:
A number, faded ink, A15429,
your great-grandfather's father, reduced to
a black armband, a yellow star.
A tattered remnant entangled among 10 feet of
Torahs piled high, sacred scrolls askew
is the life I hand you.

Blood of my blood, your blond tresses
may have saved you from the gas
I would have breathed last.
My words, my gift, surely my undoing,
all I have to offer you, to guide you
through the coming dark.
Bone of my bone, sharpen your teeth,
file down bone to spear, prepare for battle.

A brown leather-bound album is still
worshipped by those who feed on hate
like pomegranate seeds, spitting out
words like poison darts that
turn skin fair and dark alike to ash.

From the ashes you must rise,
mark your forehead in my memory and take
your place among the sisterhood reaching back
to Nefertiti, to Eve, to the Great Mother
who has no name. Like Michelangelo's *Bruges Madonna,*
The Ghent Altarpiece, Girl with a Pearl Earring, she is still
worshipped among ancient stones
once used to weigh down girls in the water
among chants of *witch*. Rise, Daughter, open your eyes
in the sunlight turning falling ash orange.

Is art worth a life?

Wear my words like a necklace, a talisman,
prayer beads you brush with your lips.
Breathe in deep and blow my words out
across the blue universe. Let them fall
like dogwood petals flowering the ashen earth.
Let your lips speak my answer.
Let your daughter sing our song.
Unsilence the bells.
Unscroll the Torahs.
In the beginning was the word.
Find your way back.
Reclaim our garden.

Return to Palmyra

To get to Palmyra, take the Superdome Exit.
U-turn at the blue shotgun two houses from the corner.
Or head northeast of Damascus where
the golden colonnaded avenue beckons, where
caravan camels spit into the thicket,
christening a salamander the color of sand
beneath palms holding up the moon, where
a withered olive tree bears witness.

Careen across the serpentine river
into the Big Easy where pedicabs hover,
gleam of wax in the wet black morning,
wisp of smoke wafting from levees.
(It was never that easy.)

Green medians laced with purple beads
invite tourists from western New York State.
Empire Exit 43 finds the "Queen of Canal Towns"
whistling Dixie beneath the Temple of Baal
over carved cypress tables scented with pine boughs.
Click. Pythia smiles through the bones,
laughter like champagne bubbles rising to the rafters.
Rooftops tip into Katrina's waters.
Atoll palm fronds whisper benediction
over washed-out coral. If you feel lost,
the fossils point the way.

One Palmyra Christmas

The carved cypress table scented with pine boughs is weighed down
with Christmas feast remains, a turkey carcass.
We can see each other smiling through the bones.
Laughter like champagne bubbles rises to the rafters.
We recline in our dining chairs, reluctant
to leave the table. Adult siblings chatter,
tongues loosened by crimson-filled goblets.
Dad loosens his belt and belts out tunes from *Cabaret*
like he was an original member of the Rat Pack, a Norse Sammy Davis, Jr.
Watching my estranged parents making nice amid the revelry,
I grin like a Cheshire Cat through the turkey bones at my sister
who winks at me this first Christmas in our shared shotgun
on Palmyra Street, New Orleans, Mid-City, the first home
either of us has ever known, a miracle we celebrate,
wiping the slate clean of childhoods spent
homeless or in foster homes, absent parents
who never quite got it together.

Dinner conversation waning, Dad ducks out
for the corner bar, an old haunt
I do not hold against him—even though—
for the final time—he never returns.
Mother becomes our new roommate—
a surprise Christmas gift I don't know
to appreciate until it is nearly too late,
her dying year filled with stories
I never thought to ask about. Her skin
sallow with disease turns the color of
the carved cypress table. She ladles out
her life to her daughters, the legacy
of loss her last words in an antiseptic hospital room
against her wishes. Mother loved that old shotgun,
the cypress table and mantle in the dining room.

She would read in her favorite easy chair
dime novels by the dozen, sometimes snoring off
to waken and say, "Do you remember?" Off
we would go back to a Christmas Day
when—if only for a matter of hours
bruised hearts unbent—
and peace reigned among turkey remains.

Watching Blue Jays Forage on All Souls' Day

Sapphire-colored scalawags scamper among squirrels,
squawk at each other, on the hunt,
chill wind an omen of coming winter.
Naked branches held up by birds drop
a sloppy squirrel. My two dachshunds dash—
the dapple grabbing a mouthful of tail.
Fast retreating squirrel chitters rebuke
all the way back up the bare tree
graced only by a gaggle of blue jays,
bluer than the sky,
bluer than my husband's eye,
the kind of blue my mother loved to wear,
refusing black, "the color of death,"
she said, which claimed her anyway in 1996,
the same year doctors pronounced me cured.
Death passed me by, took Mother instead.

Today the souls of the dead are near.
They can speak to us, reach through the veil
between living and dead. I can blow a kiss
to my mother, the daughter God took back
from my womb, and Grandmother Mildred,
her death an absence in Mother's life
she could not fill, still reaching out years later
in morphine-induced deathbed delusion
while I stood by, witnessed her last exhale.

A Halloween baby, Mother loved the holiday,
All Souls' Day, her Ouija Board,
coffee, and even me. I left her
at fifteen, left behind the battered
furniture, bruised siblings, returned only
when needed. The family repairwoman,
I could not fix Mother's dying body.

She lived her last days with me,
an uneasy truce between us,
more words unsaid than said.
So why did she try to speak to me
the night *after* she died? Why whisper to me then?
Why haunt me still? Church bells
peel away each layer of my longing for her
coffee breath to brush my cheek in the dying
fall light's lengthening shadow.

Lighting a candle in the dusky eve
this All Souls' Day, I savor
fresh-baked soul cake, sinfully sweet,
whisper in between each bite—names,
my beloved departed—watch
through the darkening window the blue jays go
silent, the sky turn cobalt, witness
the candlelight waiver, wink out.
I smile in the new dark.
The scent of coffee enshrouds me.

A Stone's Throw

Stuffed purple elephant in her left arm, my daughter
kneels, chalks twilight with her right hand on the back
window of a dollhouse nestled in the corner of our library.
Our cat sits in the window, tail twitching, glares at
a lizard on the other side of the glass.
Across the bay, a storm walks the waves.
It is difficult to paint rain while the twilight sound of crickets
creeps into the room and frogs croak and the setting sun glints
strong as noon on a distant sandbar. There are stones in the sea
no one has ever seen. Outside in the waning light, acorns cup
the worn earth at the edge of orange-kissed waters.
A spider's slick embroidery shudders in the lone dwarf pine
among the oaks. I watch the trembling web go suddenly
still. I collect these moments, delicate,
like a carton of eggs on the edge of a countertop.
I am a shadow falling briefly across my daughter's face.
The bloodspot of a single egg is a map back to the mother.

Falling Up

A gust of wind flips up leaf skirts,
flaming heavenward. Breezy ballerinas
twirl across a blue stage sprinkled with Midas-kissed dust.
Sunlight twinkles, dispelling ragweed into jeweled skies
alive with crackling blades chasing grackles, damsels in distress.
It's a dance gone wild with spiraling gyres. Gyrating ospreys
eyeball the merriment from above.

Across the universe
otherwise known as my backyard
march yellow marigolds bursting from their borders,
gunning for the sun. Another blast of cold air
rips off the heads of bright red
bat-faced flowers. Grinning, they spin off
over roof tops, break free of gravity,
falling up.

Perhaps eternity looks this way—a funhouse mirror
dwarfing infinity into a bowl curved into itself,
a clown grin stretched across a multitude of infinities,
able to gobble up several Milky Ways in a single gulp.

And me? Well, you see—
I'm the Blue Fairy chasing Monarch butterflies
late for flight to Mexico. You'll find me,
hips gyrating into chorus-girl kicks
at heaps of leaves begging to be disturbed, re-distributed,
sent sailing back up into the sky from whence they fell.
In this alien world, I am Glinda and Elphaba,
and I clash with everything. Like the leaves
set free from earth's orbit, meteors ablaze,
I am just another case of cosmic debris
firing across the universe.

What Is True

I open your door. The roaches do not disperse.
Complacent, they meander along the walls,
trailing in and out of pictures—
Mother Mary and Baby Jesus
covered in crusted dust, cobwebs
trailing the plastic frames to the ceiling.
Webbed exoskeletons hang in silence.

You do not raise your eyes to mine.
Leaning against a particle board stand,
a cracked TV precariously perched on top,
you stand in your apartment,
shirtless, grease-stained shorts hanging
below exposed belly above bare feet
black with grime, planted
on the linoleum you study with great interest,
as if its gray surface is a clue to the puzzle of ankle-deep
scattered food wrappers, magazines, yellowed envelopes,
potato chip crumbs, rusted beer cans, and brown roaches.

You'd think after years of practice, I'd grow used to this moment.
I take it all in, step over the threshold,
think back to our childhood, the bare mattress we shared
a thin sheet over us that did not keep out the night crawlers within,
the mice scurrying without, my body spooned to yours, my whisper
in the dark in your ear spilling words, weaving tales—
the prince and princess are rescued! Not true.
Welfare warriors whisk us off time and time again
to shelters shared by other children
who taunt you for words you cannot speak,
me for words I throw freely with my fists as backup.
We are shuffled about, returned each time to the hell
you escaped in silent withdrawal, I captured in words, until you turned
eight, the age I turned my first trick. I was fourteen, already a drunk
supplied with wine by those under whom I would lie.

I had to leave or die. I walked away one night,
found a halfway house, a five and dime job, joined
night school, eventually wrote my way to college,
called you to join me. You wouldn't stay.

My arms encircle the shuddering 200-pound body
of the baby brother I could not save.
Our hands lock in a blood-grip
I will not let go.

Me, Camille, and Mr. Black

For a while I could fly backwards,
wind streaming through my hair,
my face turned up to the brief gusts
exploding with such force across the porch,
the columns creaked. Facing sometimes 60 mph winds,
my eyes went slant like a Chinawoman's,
like when my pigtails were too tight.
Hugging porch columns or telephone poles, I'd stay low,
but my feet would leave the ground and dance in the wind.
And those giant porch columns, those
thick, tubular telephone poles soon would crack
like used toothpicks in the mouth of Camille.

I was eight years old and in love
with Billy, a boy who didn't know
I could fly, didn't know I could read
better than he. Did it every day, the Bible,
one chapter at a time for old Mr. Black.
His skin was the color of his name.
He couldn't see, couldn't walk, wouldn't leave
his flat in back of the old tenement
for nothing, no storm, nobody.
He just held his Bible on his chest,
said God would provide,
and would I pray with him for lost souls
like our neighbors in the dark
long before the storm knocked out the lights.
He meant Billy's folks—white trash and mean
enough to break the necks of kittens
we found abandoned under the house.

Like Mr. Black's ancestors, Camille had come
from the coast of Africa to the Mississippi Valley.
In her winds he said he could hear
screaming like so many lost souls.
Yowling loud as an angry cat, Camille swiped,
and off the ground flew all the grand houses
along Mississippi's Gulf Coast long before Katrina.
Camille's claws shredded our roof shingles in New Orleans,
batted them off into space, maybe all the way to Bogalusa
where flash floods and landslides wiped out the crops.
On my battery radio, I could barely hear wisps of news
between the wind gusts that slammed
the front porch where I'd run away from Mr. Black
gasping about the Great Emancipation finally taking place.

All I knew was that holding on to the bannister
with the thin, white arms of an eight-year-old
nobody missed, I could turn my face to the wind,
lean my body into a good gust, and
backwards
fly.

Shopping Day

That day, despite the sun beckoning me outdoors,
despite my new wireless phone and a long "to do" list,
I stayed close to the kitchen, cleaning and scrubbing surfaces
I normally ignored.

My stovetop's silvered shine
reflected my face, showed clearly my eyes go wide
when the telephone rang. I watched
my face compose itself again,
waiting until the third ring to pick up.
A man's Southern drawl breathed into my ear
invasive breast cancer.

I did not choke on my spit.
I did not pound the kitchen counter
until my knuckles bled.
I did not pick my cuticles to shreds.
I did not bite my nails.
I simply asked, "What's next?"
Switching to another self I knew
awaiting those words, I removed
me from the immediate scene,
cleaned again the gleaming stovetop.

I decided to go shopping.

Not Dillard's, not Macy's, not Saks Fifth Avenue,
no clothing stores. My body had betrayed me.
It was grocery-shopping day, my list already written.
But the betrayal ran deep.
Health foods? Why? Fresh produce? Nah.
And Winn Dixie would not do.
I was heading for Publix, the Cadillac of supermarkets—
the gourmet section, aged, marbled beef, fine wines,

a dairy and eggs aisle with mooing cows and chickens
cackling. In the delicatessen I would ingest every sample,
even the greasy cheese-filled sausages.

Jumping into my car, I drove over the speed limit,
tossed out the open window the shopping list, my coupons,
played the radio loud, let the tears blow away in the wind.

The doors of the store whooshed open for me,
nudged by the cold metal of the cart in my hands.
Instead of Budweiser, I bought Dom Perignon. Instead of Jello,
a whole New York cheesecake.
Instead of boneless, skinless chicken breasts,
I ordered ribeyes, thick-cut and bloody.
In the coffee and tea aisle, I selected
the finest Columbian beans and then moved on to the heavy cream,
but my knees weakened at the soft mooing of the cows,
and when the cackling chickens kicked in,
the aisle began to look a little crooked.
Leaning over the bright red handle of my cart,
I opened the ice cream door,
breathed deep the chilled air caressing my cheeks, concentrating,
eyes closed, separating the sounds echoing in my ears,
cackle, cackle, cancer, moo,
and something I couldn't register. Opening my eyes, I saw
a huge Coke clock above the pharmacy. Awash in red neon,
it clicked out each second, its hands collecting time
with such precision, such mechanical perfection.

Her

I have noticed, again, for the umpteenth time,
the mammogram machine's grin
looks like Ripley's Monster-Momma,
missing the alien goo, but still hungry.
       Mommy always said there were no monsters.
       No real ones. But there are.

Biting down on my right breast,
toothless, she leaves no visible bite marks. Still
the red kiss where her lips touch my skin burns,
radiates to my collar bone, licks up my neck.
       There's a monster in your chest.

I back away, glaring at her glassy grin.
Implacable, unseeing metal-bolt eyes
see right through me, through breast tissue,
through my deepest fears, the tiny crystalline babies
she knows can explode, grow
with each kiss of her plastic lips, each hiss of escaping breath
sucked up into the stale reconditioned air in which she thrives.
       It's a queen. She'll breed. You'll die.

Her head cocked just to the left, then a slight rotation,
her jaw adjusting, she gapes at me
as if surprised at my resistance. I am like a kitten
mewling in her momma's mouth, unsure
if I am about to be eaten or saved.
       I thought you were dead! Yeah. I get that a lot.

Take Two

Your kisses soft on the nape of my neck slide down to my shoulder,
tickle my collar bone, nip at my right breast.
Gently, you plant your lips in a sweet circle around
white gauze covering a new wound
where the needle went in, withdrawing flesh and blood,
in search of an old enemy.

A different breast, another mass, a new biopsy. An old fear.

I shudder at the brush of your lips and offer myself
to the wonder of your touch. Today we celebrate
a new life, released this time from the words *malignant, radiation,*
from witnessing the soft white of my breast burn red,
then turn gray as cinder ash.

I enjoy your lips like red wine, savor the flavor of your mouth.
Our bodies weave together in an old dance
made new, the giddy delight of a sentence repealed.
Together we gasp in orgasm, collapse in giggles at our inanity,
the insanity that keeps us sane
in this beautiful, deadly world
we take back daily.

Epiphany in Mississippi

I was riding shotgun in your old blue pickup
in the backwoods of Biloxi
when a snowy egret shot out of the marsh
into the sun, wings ablaze in the windshield.

You stared straight ahead into nothing,
kept driving without so much as a shift
of your blue eyes in my direction.
I blinked and the wings were gone.

But that night your eyes shined
as you gave me the egret feather found
in the backyard. We danced on the porch
despite the buzz of gnats around us in the damp,
black rain on black earth,
lightning feathering the heavens.

A thunderbolt split the sky, close,
blinding white light blasting
the dead pear tree into a single veined flame.

From the new dark edged with sparks
exploded out of the burning tree—
wings.

Eating Blackberries

Enticed by summer juice from briars
draping black over the banks of the bayou,
the prick and sting of nettles are worth
nectar dribbling down our chins like purple dew.

We savor the sweet taste our tongues share,
your mouth on mine,
free from the brambles more berries.

We eat and drink the afternoon away until you say *no more*, drawing
purple hearts on my bare skin until I am berry-stained from instep to chin.

Wet with desire at your touch, I drip like berry juice from your fingertips.

A Midsummer Night's Musings

In between cloud games and applications of Coppertone
on the summer house rooftop, your hand slipped between my thighs.
Our tongues tasted the salt seasoning each other's lips and skin
on an afternoon seared into memory.

My blue china bowl fell, cracked open, spilled bright red
crawfish rolling across the black asphalt roof shingles,
my napkin fluttering down the alley's breezeway,
settling into sandy loam on the path to the Gulf
where you could wade for what seemed like miles
in the thigh-high waters of our youthful *amour.*

Twilight, a Creamsicle sky melting into the horizon
takes me back—my fingers stroking your brown curls,
my lips a whisper in your ear in tune with the radio's
tinny "Puppy Love" ode to teenage lust.

Shadowed by the widow's peak of Grandmother's summer house,
we swapped baseball cards, kisses, stole illicit bases, delighted
that beneath us our mothers, none the wiser in afternoon heat,
alternated between dabbing brows with starched handkerchiefs
and lifting china cups of painted peonies, pinkies just so,
delicate crooks warding off bad behavior
with waves of disdain mirrored in silver servers of afternoon tea.
Meanwhile cast iron pots out back welcomed mudbugs, boiling water
turning them crimson as they cooked like us in the late afternoon sun.

Maybe if I had resisted nibbling your sun-browned ear,
we would not have faced later years of broken china
fractured in pitching contests under roofs
grown too close over bodies grown too heavy
with the baggage of the familiar. For an afternoon
on a rooftop in June we aligned our tails and teacups
into a teenaged fiction untouched by truths
we would come to know soon enough, anyway.

When Geese Fly South

Your tee shirt and uniform blues over the back of a chair
rustle in the cool breeze drifting your musk scent across
this wide bed.

Engulfed in flame
an airplane dives, dives
into the deep blue
of the small dot marking
the expiration of our ancient TV.

Silver handcuffs over chair back glimmer in the quarter moon's
slow light crossing the expanse of the white wall
embracing your father's rifle.

I rise above myself, float out the window
over the net of silver
barbed wire surrounding our farmyard.

A flock of geese make an arc above me, magnet to the hunter's aim.
We grace the sight of the blind, fly into the wind.

Discharged, a puff of smoke dissolves into the night.
I am back beside myself, you
a lean shadow beyond the light of my cigarette.

Your grandfather's gold pocket watch lies
on the nightstand, ticks off
each second of our breathing,
our lives spent under this roof
a clockwork of sirens and prayers.

The feathers in our bed, so soft and deep,
lull me to sleep in our cotton sheets,
so clean, so twisted.

The Geometry of Your Bones

Cold cigarette butts and stale beer all that's left of the party,
I'm bagging trash, but stop
to watch the question mark of your back.
You are leaning into the sudsy kitchen sink,
the window pane before you sprouting clouds
with each puff of your breath.

While I am supposed to gather soiled paper plates,
you are washing the blue china you have washed for 18 years
at that ancient porcelain sink we have shared for as long.
I complete my circuit of the house slowly
until I am back behind you
so close I could touch you
but I don't.

Stopped by the wonder of your shoulder blades,
those arrowheads of your back armor, I watch
your body speak its evidence, try to work out
the vocabulary of your silence, the delicate design of your
breath on the window, the geometry of your bones.

Still Life

While I lie awake in my sleeping husband's arms

     Veterans Highway neon red runs to orange horizon, breaks

in our brick colonial suburb

     where the sun sits on the back of the day

my sister loses herself, her farmhouse disappearing in a flashback.

     drifting through the door of a one-room sweatbox

Her husband coaxes her out of closets

     where my family lives, looks after Father, five feet two,

nights their baby daughter turns

     all stubble and whistle. When I walk in, their eyes shift

from diamond to coal on a road running

     to a bathroom's closed door.

back to Veterans Highway.

     My sister cries, miscarries the result of her latest rape.

I hear her whimper in the hot wind's rattle

     She won't let me in, back in this place I left,

through my bedroom window.

     this place I've never left.

I stare into the night

No matter the states I put between me,

whispering, I'm here, but I know we're both back

faded store fronts, bruised vaginas, broken ribs

on a buckled street in a sweltering room.

behind barred windows protecting nothing.

Black nights my sister cries, I scream awake,
throat raw, hands clawed, sheets wet
with anger that won't wash out, won't be
held in a man's arms.

Oh

I'm a powerful man, big connections,
my father bellows, throws down his beer can,
glares at me to fetch
his seventh beer of a night barely dark,
blue-black clouds crowding the window's
cracked glass, hurricane deadeye
at river's mouth. Swamped fishing-boat
splinters wash across the levee,
close. I cross myself, turn,
pitch him a can,
jump back fast.

Sprawled in the middle of his soiled corner
mattress, his shrunken frame still
bigger than me, he sinks in his Salvation
Army jacket doubling as a blanket. Damp
air builds the squall around us.
Pop goes the beer tab. My shoulders jerk.
Fingers curled, I breathe
deep the fetid air, make ready.

He shifts, farts, looks at me deadeye.
Don't look down.

Sudden wind slams against the wall
seagulls' thin screams.

Drowning gasp for air, open-mouthed.
There is no air, no water.

Stalemate

At fourteen, oozing hormones
across the chessboard, I leaned
toward you, a *Con Thien* veteran
seven years my senior.

Legless, heavy artillery there, you met
protest here. Nobody but me seemed to care
to know you. A curious girl, I was
passionate for lost causes.

Gunfire erupting from the burned-out building
across the street, your dealer a dim shadow
slips from the corner of my tired eye
at window's edge. Years later
I watch you twitch, your eyes glazed over
by another dime bag of man-made snow,
your escape from the heat, the Vietnamese
rice paddies you see rising among the rusted
skeletons on the Detroit backstreets we still haunt.

Noises waft in the yawning window
through which you repeat you want to jump.
Smoothing my thumbnail along your eyebrow,
I whisper in your ear, *you can't jump,*
a stale joke we've shared for too long.

Losing at chess again, I finger victory
for you, surrender a game
neither of us won.

Year of the Rat

I stare at the skeletal rattling I've pinned in a corner
who'd hidden behind a nest of unwashed clothes.
I offer my bottle of bourbon; spill a drop or two,
drink a toast, take aim at his boney head.

His black eyes lock with mine. I don't let loose.
Defiant fear, a common bond, flares,
strikes between us like a damp match.
We're both gray matter taking up space.

Rat shudders, collapses, dead—just like that.
I shake my head. No fanfare. No farewell.
Nobody knows but me. I sing a verse
from Sunday School (another life I knew
of sunning laundry, sweet milk, fresh baked bread).
I bless us both in Old Crow's amber drops.

Fresh Cuttings

The sun already a blister in the bright blue haze,
Daffodils melt in the retreat of late spring.
In our garden's yellow nodding we snip away,
tuck the best blooms in our baskets,
your baseball cap bobbing above a sea of flowers.

Tulips burn red in shafts of yellow light
slicking through pine trees. You shade your eyes, blink
in the bright light that's burst open.
A small cloud passes between us. My basket
grows heavy on my arm. The cuttings
wink at me, pink and yellow
blooms for the dinner table.
I want to put down my basket,
make you see the matchstick
forearms, the tracks
I can still trace
meant to keep away lurking shadows.
You won't see them.

Our garden feeds on the rich ash of last night.
We watched the fire consume
the cord of wood kept burning
despite water in the logs threatening
to douse your efforts at romance—the sheepskin rug,
champagne, glasses tipped against the spreading dark.

I hear voices whisper in the wind sighing through the pines.
Their intensity rises and falls like the sun
shearing the hedges looped around the daffodils.
The tulips swoon, look like limp ropes at the feet of the trees,
like the one behind the garage workbench.
who wants a garden in a world not condemned.

You come to me, hold your face close to mine. I can see
in your eyes my face, the woman you love,
the woman who loves the earth in her hands,

We turn our backs to the trees,
walk back through the garden.
Among the stalks stroking our knees
are the bright borders of Basket-of-Gold,
the spreading cushion of flowers that combines so well
with Forget-Me-Not and Blue Phlox and Buttercup.
Sweet Alyssum nods benediction in the late morning breeze.

After growing up in New Orleans, Louisiana, **Katherine Nelson-Born** met the love of her life in Pensacola, Florida, where she lives and teaches English and American literature and consults for K & K Manuscript Editing. Her poems have appeared in *AlaLit.com*, *the Birmingham Poetry Review, Emerald Coast Review, Excelsior ReView, GSU Review, Longleaf Pine, Maple Leaf Rag* and *Penumbra*.

Her poetry has a bittersweet grounding in her childhood and New Orleans roots, seasoned with her survival of hurricanes, breast cancer, and lost loved ones and flavored with a fierce determination to live life to its fullest. Katherine has previously won the University of New Orleans *Ellipsis* award for poetry, placed twice among finalists in the Agnes Scott College Writer's Festival, and was awarded honorable mention at the 2015 Fairhope Alabama Writers' Conclave.

Katherine Nelson-Born resides in Pensacola's lovely East Hill neighborhood and is a long-time member of the West Florida Literary Federation. She is an active member of her community, whether promoting creative writing or the preservation of the planet her daughter inherits.